OUTDOOR Math

Fun Activities for Every Season

Emma AdBåge

Kids Can Press

What Are Numbers?

Look around you! Numbers are everywhere. They are in the hundreds of leaves crunching under your feet and in the pair of birds flying high in the sky.

Numbers are like a math alphabet. You need them to count, just as you need letters to read and write.

Each number represents a different amount.

ZERO = Clouds in the sky on a clear, sunny day.

ONE = You! There's only one in the world.

TWO = Ends on a worm, wiggling in the dirt.

THREE = Dogs in the family, when a dad dog and a mom dog have a puppy. So cute!

FOUR = Legs on a horse. That's why it can run so fast!

FIVE = Arms on a starfish, clinging to a rock.

 SIX = Legs on a beetle. Watch it scurry away.

SEVEN = Colors in a rainbow: red, orange, yellow, green, blue, indigo and violet.

 EIGHT = Feet on a spider. Look at all his teeny-tiny shoes!

NINE = Bandages on your toes, when you've stubbed all of them … except for one.

 TEN = Fingers in your new woolly red gloves. So warm!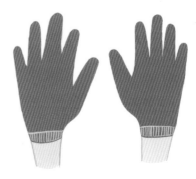

3

SPRING MATH

Treasure hunt

You'll need: paper, a pencil, paint in different colors, a paintbrush

Everyone draws a simple map of the yard or playground and collects 6 different treasures — maybe sticks or stones. Paint the treasures the same color so they are easy to identify. Then hide them outside and mark the spots on your map with an X. Swap maps with your friends. The one who finds the most treasures wins!

Worm measure

You'll need: a ruler

When the spring rain falls, the worms come out to play! Carefully collect some worms and measure their lengths using a ruler. Which one is longest? Which is shortest? If you line them up end to end, how long are they together? Don't forget to return your worms to the dirt when you're done!

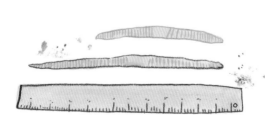

Simple coordinates

You'll need: paper, a pencil

Draw a grid with 4 columns and 4 rows. Number the columns along the top, and label the rows with letters down the left side. Now each box has a name, or coordinate, where the number and letter meet: A1, D3 and so on.

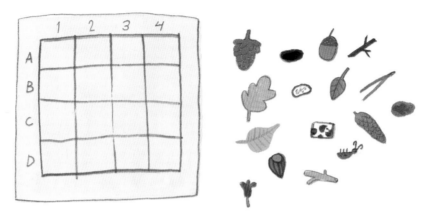

Head outside to collect at least 16 objects from nature. Make sure you have some variety — such as different kinds of leaves or different-colored stones. Decide what kind of objects go in each box. For example, only white stones go in A4 and acorns go in D3. Then place all of your objects in the correct boxes. Which box has the most? Which box has the fewest?

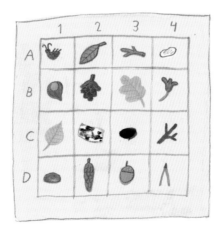

Shake hands

On a sunny day, walk around and shake hands with, or high five, a group of friends. How many handshakes or high fives are possible with only 2 people? How about with a group of 3? Or 4 or 5? Try it out!

One-minute challenge

You'll need: a stopwatch, rain boots

After a rainstorm, find a nice big puddle. How many times can you jump up and down in it in 1 minute? Ask a friend to time you while you keep count. (Remind him to stand back so he doesn't get splashed!) Ready, set, go!

Free form

You'll need: one 5-meter (16-foot) rope per group

Find a spot outside where there is lots of space. Divide into groups of 4 or more people. Each group gets a rope and ties the ends together, and everyone holds on to the rope with at least one hand. Practice making different shapes with the rope.

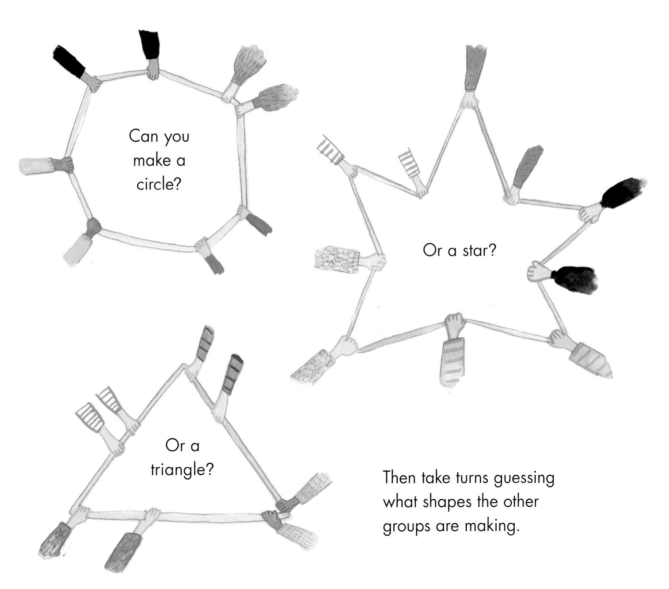

Can you make a circle?

Or a star?

Or a triangle?

Then take turns guessing what shapes the other groups are making.

SUMMER MATH

Bottle bowling

You'll need: 10 empty plastic bottles with caps, paper, a marker, tape, a ball

Fill the plastic bottles halfway with sand or water. (Be sure to tighten the caps well!) With the paper, marker and tape, label each bottle from 1 to 10 — that's how many points the bottle is worth.

Find a space outside and set up the bottles like bowling pins, then grab a ball and start bowling! Roll the ball toward the bottles. Each player gets 2 turns to knock over as many as possible. Write down and add up the points for each bottle knocked down. Then reset the bottles for the next player. Who will knock down the most bottles and earn the most points?

Cloud count

Lie on your back in the grass and count the clouds in the sky. How many clouds can you see? On a hot summer day, you'll notice that the clouds get smaller and smaller until they disappear. And some clouds change shape, combine with other clouds or divide into separate clouds. After a few minutes, count them again. Are there more clouds? Or fewer? How many more or fewer are there than before?

The thief

You'll need: a die

Find a partner and collect 10 objects each, such as shells from the beach or stones — whatever you can find! Place your objects in front of you. One person rolls the die and steals that number of objects from her partner. Then switch, so the other person rolls the die and gets to steal back. Keep going until someone runs out of objects. The person who steals them all wins.

Pinecone math

To get ready for winter, squirrels collect and store pinecones and other seeds. Working with a group of friends, collect 10 pinecones each. Now figure out how many everyone has gathered. Then place them all in a pile and see how high it gets!

Stone toss

With a friend or in a group, collect 5 small
stones, chestnuts or other hard objects from nature.
Now find a big tree. With a stick, draw a line in the
dirt a good distance from the tree — not too close,
but not too far. Make sure everyone is standing behind
the line. Then take turns throwing your objects at the
trunk. Each time you hit
the tree, you get 1 point.
Who has the best shot?

Pattern play

You'll need: chalk (optional)

Draw a long grid, separated into 5 boxes, using a stick in the dirt
or chalk on the pavement. Make a series of patterns with acorns or
leaves or other objects from nature, adding 2 more objects to the
pattern in each box. Leave the last box in the grid empty. Have a
friend guess what pattern comes next!

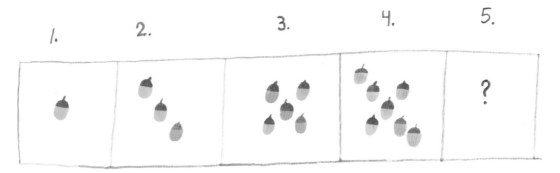